Vitória É Certa | Niyi Borire

VITÓRIA É CERTA

The Roadmap to Peace and Triumph In Trying Times

Niyi Borire

Vitória É Certa

© Niyi Borire 2021

All rights reserved.

No part of this publication may be reproduced, distributed, or transmitted in any form or by any means, including photocopying, recording, or any other electronic or mechanical method, without the prior written permission of the author, except in the case of brief quotations embodied in critical reviews and certain other non-commercial uses permitted by copyright law.

All scripture quotations are taken from the King James Version (KJV) except otherwise stated.

Dedication

To every man and woman who is underrated, undervalued, and underestimated.

To those who are constantly forgotten, overlooked, and unnoticed.

To that young person who is drowning and overwhelmed by the deluge of these trying times.

Though the billows may roll, you will not be buried below.

Acknowledgments

It's always a privilege to be a channel through which God blesses His people. I am grateful to God – the source of my inspiration – who has counted me worthy to share these truths with my generation and the one to come. Thank You, Lord.

I appreciate my mentees, Grace and Mary. Thanks for allowing me to be a blessing to you just as you are a blessing to me. I believe in you and I am persuaded that your lives will bless your generation tremendously.

Thank you, Sam Adetiran – my editor – for your expertise and benignity all through the process that turned the series of messages I taught in church to this book that will now bless many lives. God bless you.

Finally, I am grateful to God for the gift of a good wife. Thank you, my dear Olayemi, for standing with me, for me, and by me all these years. It's so beautiful to know that we have been enjoying victory together in life by practicing the principles I have shared in this book. I love you and will always be blessed to have you.

Contents

Dedication iii

Acknowledgments iv

Contents v

Introduction vi

    Chapter 1 - PERSISTENCE 10

    Chapter 2 - POWER 37

    Chapter 3 - PASSION 60

    Chapter 4 - PURITY 73

    Chapter 5 - PEACE 85

    Chapter 6 - PRAISE 99

    Chapter 7 - CONCLUSION: THE VICTORY THAT OVERCOMES 103

Vitória É Certa | Niyi Borire

Introduction

If there is something about life that most people dread, it is uncertainty. Many people will gladly pay if there was a fee attached to eradicating uncertainty in life. How beautiful would it be if you can always predict what happens in your life every day? Wouldn't it even be nicer to realise that you don't have to face any negative occurrence and just coast through the sea of life like a master glider?

I wish I could tell you that you will never have troubles or face difficulties in life but even Jesus couldn't do that. This is what He said, *'These things I have spoken to you, that in me ye might have peace. In the world ye shall have tribulation: but be of good cheer; I have overcome the world'* (John 16:63). The Almighty Jesus was speaking to His disciples here. He made them see that in the world there would be uncertainties (things that would get you unsettled and doubtful like tribulations). However, something is certain even in the midst of uncertainty - VICTORY.

For the believer in Christ, there is certainty even in the midst of uncertainty. He is assured of victory before the battles he will face because his Saviour has won the victory on his behalf already. That is so assuring. The believer is the only warrior that always fights a battle that is already won. Because Jesus overcame, the believer is an overcomer.

The twist, however, is that many believers are not winning all of their life battles and that really breaks the heart of Jesus. How can you suffer for what has already been paid for? The victory the believer has doesn't preclude him from fighting, it only assures him of victory. The challenge is that most times, the believer fails because he is not putting up a fight at all or he is fighting with the wrong mindset. Nobody wins a fight where he is already defeated in his mind.

We already have the victory in Christ but the devil will not stop assaulting us. He is a bully and bullies are not nice at all. The battles we fight as believers must be won by appropriation - enforcing the victory that is already ours. Battles are fought with weapons. However, a man with a superior weapon that he doesn't know how to use can still be defeated by a man who is very good at using his inferior weapon. This is exactly how the devil floors believers most of the time. He understands that many of us are not skillful in using our weapon - our faith. for everyone born of God overcomes the world. *'This is the victory that has overcome the world, even our faith'.* (1 John 5:4 NIV)

Faith is the potent weapon that wins the victory for the believer always. However, faith doesn't work in isolation. *'For whatever things were written before were written for our learning, that through perseverance and through encouragement of the Scriptures we might have hope'.* (Romans 15:4 WEB). Here, we see that perseverance is needed to keep hope alive. Without hope, you can't keep fighting. Hebrews 6:12 puts it this way, *'So don't allow your hearts to grow dull or lose your enthusiasm, but follow the example of those who fully received what God has promised because of their strong faith and patient endurance'.* (Hebrews 6:12 TPT). We cannot obtain the victory God has promised us if we are not patient.

What this book is all about is to show you that your victory is certain (vitória é certa - in Portuguese). It's a done deal! However, you need to enforce your victory through your faith. The first six chapters focus on the things that must accompany your faith (persistence, power, passion, purity, peace, and praise). The last chapter focuses on the victory that overcomes - our faith.

It's my prayer that as you read through the pages of this book, the eyes of your understanding will be enlightened to the fact that victory is already yours, and your heart will be strengthened to appropriate that victory every day of your life, no matter what comes your way.

Niyi Borire.

1
PERSISTENCE

When you hear the word, surviving time, the first thing that probably comes to your mind is a person sentenced to life imprisonment, and you are wondering how that person will survive or how he will spend his time. That's not the route I will be taking you through.

Before I go deeper into surviving time, I need to explain the concept of change. Change is a constant phenomenon in life. Change occurs with time. Change is a natural phenomenon that cannot be stopped. Now, the reality is that a lot of the time when change occurs, we are oblivious to it in the actual sense of it. For instance, if you take a picture of who you were ten years ago and compare it with who you are now, you would notice a change in your physical appearance. Hence, change is something that is bound to happen.

The problem some of us face is that when change happens, we lose quality, we lose our values, we lose the essence of our lives. So, how can we survive and stand firm in our faith and identity in Christ even though we are going through change? That is what we will be considering in this chapter.

Change is a natural order. C.S. Lewis said, *'Isn't it funny how day by day nothing changes but when you look, everything is changed'* Is that not correct? My first son is a ten-year-old boy and sometimes I wonder how he got as tall as he is now. How did that happen? He has grown without my being conscious of it and this is simply because we live together. You probably have experienced that too when you see someone you have not seen in a long time and they look so different. They have changed. You are able to immediately sense or appreciate that change because you have not seen them in a while.

Well, change happens every day even though we are not very keen to pick it out. You are not the person you were ten years ago. Things change. Our experiences change. We find new relationships. We change jobs. We get more exposure. We meet new people. We join a new church. We make new friends. It's natural for change to happen. Every time, we are in a constant state of change. And there is nothing we can do to stop change. Change is happening even when you cannot perceive it.

Recently, I wanted to pick something that my kids put under the furniture and I felt a little crack in my back, and I was like, '*Woohoo! I am changing.*' I immediately understood that my body was changing. Change is inevitable. There are four key things about change:

1. **Identity**: Your identity is who you are and leads to how you define yourself. Your identity is not synonymous with your career, professional qualifications, or any other title. It is the core of your person. Your identity is based on God's definition. Our true identity is our identity in Christ. Whoever He says we are is who we are, regardless of our frailties and failures. So, if you ask me who I am I will say,

    I am the son of the living God. I am redeemed. I am protected. I am forgiven. I am loved.

2. **Purpose**: This is 'why' you are who you are. It is why God designed you the way you are. It is why you are tall, big, quiet, outspoken, etc. It is also

why you have your emotional characteristics, temperament, etc. Your purpose is hidden in your design. It is the reason why you do things in a way that is different from how others do them.

Purpose was the original plan of God for you which is more detailed than the overall plan of God for every man (getting saved and spreading the glory of God over the earth). God has a specific purpose for everyone. There is something He has enabled you to contribute. Your purpose is connected to your identity.

3. **Assignment**: Your assignment is what you do. It is time-bound. They are those tasks, jobs, and responsibilities God will bring your way. Your assignment is often incremental and progressive. For instance, Joseph's overall purpose was to deliver the children of Israel from the famine, however, he had different assignments (tasks) to attend to (in Potiphar's house, the prison, etc.) on his way to that ultimate purpose.

If you think back, you will remember how you served in certain capacities at different times E.g. When you were a cell leader or worked in a certain industry, etc. I am a firm believer in the truth that work is ministry. At times, our assignments don't directly relate to the ultimate plan God has for us. Joseph would probably have wondered about what going to jail had to do with becoming the leader that would help set his people free. A lot of us find ourselves in uncomfortable assignments, however, they have a part to play in the bigger picture. Many of us have had to change jobs at different times. Assignments are like bus stops in life but some of us build mansions where we should just have been sojourners.

4. **Culture**: This is how you live your life. It's a manifestation of who you are and a combination of your ideas, values, social behaviour, how you dress, what you eat, how you engage in your social interactions, etc. Culture is passed from generation to generation. It is formed by exposure to experiences, people, and so on. It works by observation many times, so it is not always a conscious teaching process.

There is the story of a man who asked his wife why she always cut the head and tail of a fish before frying and she said she didn't know, it was just how she saw her mother do it. Then the wife decided to ask her mother who also didn't know because that was how the grandmother was doing it. The mother also asked the grandmother who revealed that it was because the frying pan was too small for the fish (in her days) that she adopted that style of cutting the head and tail of a fish before frying.

Culture influences us either by observation or instruction. Learning can be through experience, observation, or teaching. These processes impact our memories and in turn alter our habits, behavioural patterns, attitudinal changes, that will eventually form our culture.

Our lives revolve around these four concepts. These concepts are subject to change and the person who can master change is the one that will succeed. Our culture can influence our identity and vice versa, and our purpose will reflect in our assignment. However, it is worthy to note that though our culture may change, our identity should not change. Our purpose can be altered by our decisions or choices. Many people abandon their purpose for financial security. It doesn't mean God's purpose for them has changed but they can change it by how they relate to it. Abraham went down to Egypt during the famine in his time, however, God told Isaac to remain in the land where there was a famine during his time. He sowed in that same land and reaped a hundredfold. Our purpose does not change but we can walk away from it by our decisions or actions.

How we live may change but who we are must not. This is because how we live our lives depends on a lot of external factors that are beyond us. For instance, there was no social media 20 years ago. Most of us had no mobile phones. I remember those days when I had to go to call centres and pay to call my girlfriend then. Sometimes, there will be a long queue and I have to say '*I love you darling*' on that queue regardless of who was listening. There was no WhatsApp or any chatting platform then. I remember sharing with some people recently that I was very good at writing love letters then – two to three pages. I was so confident in my writing that I believed any girl who reads my letters will have a rethink even if she already had a boyfriend. What I am driving at is that culture changes. Who has the time to be writing such long letters these days? Now, an emoji can communicate your love and the person gets you.

Also, when I was in High School, guys were coaching me on how to woo a lady. We say things like, '*Hello, lady. I want to be your B and I want you to be my G*'. I remember vividly how I will rehearse and cram my lyrics in the bathroom. The only time I tried approaching a lady to recite my lyrics, I froze and I had to change the conversation to academics, '*Oh, how was the Maths class? The teacher is very good. I will see you later, bye*'. Nothing about love could come out of my mouth. I think it's a bit easier these days. You may see a guy bump into a lady and say, '*I fall for you*' and the lady will respond, '*Oh, that is romantic, can I have your number?*' Culture changes. The way we do things changes. The way we speak, interact changes. Our ideas change. There was a time women could not do certain things because they were reserved for men.

The problem for Christians is when we let our identity change because of the changes around us. That's where I am going. The victorious Christian is one who will not lose his identity in a changing world. He is that person who can stand to say no even when the world says yes as long as the yes is contrary to God's Word. So, when culture changes, as a Christian, you know who You have believed and you stand your ground to affirm that you are saved, renewed, and belong to Jesus. You affirm that your relationship with God is not directed or influenced by what happens in society. Your relationship with Jesus is so tight that even if the world changes, it does not move you.

Going back to relationships, in those days, we approached women through an intermediary. You dare not go on your own, first. You either go through the parents or someone close to her. The interesting part is that some of the marriages initiated this way have stood the test of time. However, these days, you just swipe left and swipe right on your phone and meet the lady somewhere. It took a long process those days but now it is one swipe away. The culture has changed. Nonetheless, the principles guiding the identity of a Christian have not changed. The fact that you should keep your marital bed holy will not change. In the years past, Christian brothers could disguise themselves as someone else (so that no one will recognise them) and sneak to buy dirty magazines but today no one needs to sneak anywhere, they are all on mobile devices. But because you know who you are in Christ Jesus, even though all those pleasurable stuff is readily accessible to you, you don't compromise. Even when you are served nasty things on a platter of gold, you choose not to accept or do them because you know who you are in Christ.

Those who will succeed and overcome in this generation are those who will persist despite the changing culture. They will not lose their identity. They are not people seeking popularity or worldly approval.

They are content with maintaining their individuality; people who are not ashamed to confess their belief in Jesus.

Our assignments will change from time to time as I stated earlier. We must not fall into the trap of turning our assignments to our purpose as most people do. Your purpose is the grandmaster plan that God has for you but He will sometimes take you through certain processes in life, not because that is where your destination is. If you are not sensitive to why God is taking you through where He is taking you, you may be building mansions where you are not meant to. It may feel pleasurable staying there but it may not be in God's grand plan for your life that you stay there.

My prayer for you is that God will give you a revelation of who you are and why you are who you are. When you know who you are, you won't be moved by what others are doing, and when you know why you are who you are, you won't sit down with what you are doing now as though that is who you are.

Ruth was a Moabite who followed Naomi after they had both lost their husbands. Though Naomi urged her to go back, Ruth said to her, *'Your people will be my people'*. Do you know what that means? Ruth was saying she was ready to change her culture. So, there are times when we just must change our culture, and we all do this. On Monday mornings, some of us change our voices and style of speaking on the phone (when we don't know who is calling) perhaps because our work demands it or we are simply trying to impress. Yes, sometimes we have to adapt but in adapting, we must not lose our identities. Our assignments also may change but we must not lose our sense of purpose.

For instance, you may temporarily change the purpose of a glass table that was designed to hold a glass of water or a light material (like a book) to a chair that can support your weight but that doesn't change its original purpose. So, there may be times in your life when your table becomes a chair but don't turn a table into a chair because that was not what it was designed to do. You must understand this. Whether it is in a relationship, your job, or the suburb you live in, God will bring you into some circumstances that are meant to build you but they are not meant to be your final destination. You must be sensitive to this.

A victorious person is someone who is able to maintain their identity and purpose despite the changes in their culture and assignment. This is achieved through persistence. Victory can only be sustained by persistence. Persistence is staying power. Persistence is the result of the revelation of your identity and purpose. Why will you stay where you are? It's because God has opened your eyes to see who you are and why you are who you are. This helps you to stay when others are running around because you are seeing something that they are not seeing. I love to use my marriage as an example here. A lot of people did not believe in our relationship when it started but we both believed in it. Sometimes, God will give you an idea, revelation, inspiration, etc. that other people will not believe in. Because they cannot see what you have seen, they will attempt to minimise and trivialise the value of what you have. However, you stay with it because you have seen it and believe it.

God told Abraham to leave his father's house to a land He will show him. As a father, if my son says he is leaving, I will ask him where his destination is. I will require that he shows me on Google map. That action of making an attempt to leave for a place that you don't know will be strange to anyone today. We probably will think the person is schizophrenic and perhaps need the attention of a psychiatrist. But Abraham did just that. He left by faith. God will ask you to leave your comfort zone. God will tell you to leave a comfortable job and start something new. God will tell you to leave that comfortable relationship to start relating with someone much younger than you in experience but when you know it is God, you do it. Persistence happens when you know you have seen the end from the beginning. It happens when God gives you a glimpse of where He is taking you. People who give up easily on their dreams are people who have not seen it or those who live other people's dreams.

The woman with the issue of blood knew that she wanted something from Jesus so she pushed against the press. There was a revelation of what she could get. She was probably anaemic from her loss of blood. She was weak but she had a picture in mind – to get healed by touching Jesus' garment. Hence, she pushed against all odds.

ERASED

There are three principles by which the identity of a person should be defined:

Nucleus: By the core or content of the individual. This refers to the core personality of a person, who they truly are.

Traits: By the character or conduct of the person. These are specific characteristics, qualities, or attributes that make an individual different from others.

Interests: The things or courses you identify yourself with. We assume different positions for different things. For instance, I am someone who loves sports. I have a football club I support in England. I have their jersey and support the club even though none of the members of the team knows me. Some other people identify themselves by their religious affiliations.

There can be no new identity if there was no old identity. What makes the new new is because there was an old. To understand the new identity of a Believer, we must first understand the old identity. The old identity is the floored human nature (Adamic) that we were all born with. We are naturally programmed to sin.

'Once you were dead because of your disobedience and your many sins. You used to live in sin, just like the rest of the world, obeying the devil – the commander of the powers in the unseen world. He is the spirit at work in the hearts of those who refuse to obey God. All of us used to live that way, following the passionate desires and inclinations of our sinful nature. By our very nature we were subject to God's anger just like everyone else'. Ephesians 2:1-3 (NLT)

Ephesians 2:1 describes the old identity of every believer (or even unbeliever). The nucleus of the old identity is **being dead** – separation from God. That is the core of the old man. There is no life in it. **Living in** sin was the trait of the old identity. It obeyed the devil rather than God. It was sinful. **The interests** of the old identity were to follow the inclination of the flesh – satisfying the flesh.

At salvation, when a man comes to the knowledge of Christ, the man becomes renewed – born again. Salvation ushers us into a new identity in Christ. We become a part of God's family. We are branded with Christ. The Word of God shapes us into this new person (1 Peter 1:21).

'But God is so rich in mercy, and he loved us so much, that even though we were dead because of our sins, he gave us life when he raised Christ from the dead.' (Ephesians 2:4-5 NLT). The nucleus of the new identity is **life.** *'For we are God's masterpiece. He has created us anew in Christ Jesus, so we can do the good things he planned for us long ago'*. (Ephesians 2:10 NLT) The very substance of the new identity is full of the life of God. It is operational already.

The trait of the new identity is **doing good things.** We now do things that honour God. Our conduct and behaviour bring glory to God. We manifest good things. Our life is a reflection of the image of God.

'For he raised us from the dead along with Christ and seated us with him in the heavenly realms because we are united with Christ Jesus.' (Ephesians 2:6 NLT)

The interest of the new identity is **united with Christ**. Your mind is now aligned with that of Christ. When you have a new identity, all you want to do is to bring glory to God.

CHRIST THE ERASER

To erase something is to abolish, eliminate, negate, obliterate, wipe out, strikeout, cut out, take out, efface, expunge, nullify something. God is the One who erases our bad identity. People can change their identity, naturally, for different reasons. For example, a criminal can erase his identity to evade justice or punishment but that cannot erase his criminal record. Changing identity in the natural doesn't erase a criminal record but thanks be to the Lord Jesus Christ who is our Eraser.

'He cancelled the record of the charges against us and took it away by nailing it to the cross' Colossians 2:14 NLT

When you come into union with Christ and you accept the new identity, the criminal record of your old life is cancelled by Christ. Jesus Christ is an expert in erasing criminal records. Every legal indebtedness we had as a result of our past life is erased by Jesus. Jesus makes all things new for us.

'There is therefore now no condemnation to them which are in Christ Jesus, who walk not after the flesh, but after the Spirit' (Romans 8:1 NLT)

What Our New Identity Confers on Us

1. **A new Creation**: In Christ Jesus, what matters is that we have a new life. We become a new creation. (Corinthians 5:17, Galatians 6:15, Romans 6:4)
2. **A new Covenant**: We begin to operate under a new covenant (Matthew 28:16, Hebrews 12:24)
3. **A new Citizenship**: We become citizens of God's kingdom (Ephesians 2:19)
4. **A new Commandment**: We operate by a new commandment now and that is the commandment of love (John 13:34)

Who we are in Christ (our new identity) is a means, not an end in itself. God is our all-satisfying end. God has given us a new identity so that His identity can be proclaimed through us. Our identity in Christ must reflect God's love because God is love. The essence of our identity is that the excellency of God is revealed in us.

BE IMMOVABLE!

'Therefore my beloved brethren, be ye steadfast, unmoveable, always abounding in the work of God...' (1 Corinthians 15:58)

The word unmovable or immovable does not exist without the word, *move* So, when God says to you to be immovable, He is saying so because there is the tendency to move. He is not asking people who cannot be moved to be immovable. How can you tell the owner of a business to be unsackable? It's not possible! You can only tell an employee to be unsackable. So, you don't tell someone to move when they don't have the tendency to do so.

There are forces that are trying to move us. We need to understand those forces, situations, and concepts that try to move us. If you don't understand the forces trying to move you, you cannot understand why you should be immovable and how to resist those forces. Below are six forces that can move us:

1. **Failure**: This is a force that can move people. People don't want to associate with a brand that is not high up there or succeeding. People go away from an association, church, organisation, company, etc. that is not succeeding. Real fans don't stop believing in a team even when they are losing year in year out. It's painful, but they stay with their beloved club. Failure is a force that can move us away from our position, purpose, or identity. We must understand that failure is important for our growth. Proverbs 24:16 says the righteous shall fall seven times and rise again. The glory of Christianity is not in not falling but rising. Every time you fail, you must understand that it is an opportunity for growth. I have never failed an exam in my life.

    My first taste of failure in the academic world was during my Ph.D. when I submitted the first chapter of my thesis for publication and it was rejected with an emphasis. I couldn't believe it. After all the research I had carried out with sleepless nights. I went back to review it, kept writing, and put in more work. I was determined to succeed. While on it, this time, I realised that I got to understand the technique better. My third chapter was accepted in a worldwide journal. That paper that I wrote was so novel that I won an award. I was the third Australian to win that award. I was flown (Business Class) to Philips Arizona to present my paper in front of a world-class audience. When I got to the hotel where I was lodged, it was a resort. I had to do a video call with my wife just for her to see where they put me. After the speech, I was given 2000 USD.

I could have given up after that first attempt. Up till now, I am the first person to apply the technique I used for the patient population the research was based on. You have to make up your mind to stand firm despite failure.

2. **Family and friends**: Sometimes, the opinion of family and friends may want to move us away from our purpose. Our family and friends may not understand what we have seen. The journey to your purpose is an individual journey. Joseph had a dream that none of his siblings understood. Sometimes, those closest to us are the ones that will try to abort God's dream for our lives. They want us to live our lives according to their

judgement or estimation and move us away from God's plan. You have to grow a spine to stand your ground based on what God is saying to you per time.

3. **Finances**: The pressure of finance often pushes us away from our dreams. God will often give you a dream that is bigger than you. And as long as you stay there, He will finance that dream or vision. It is not a God-given dream if it is something you can do on your own. It is God-given because you need to depend on Him. Therefore, you've got to lean on God and learn to trust Him. Don't be quick to move to what will give you the quickest money. Some people always want to join the people that have the biggest money. You must resist the pressure of finances.

I remember one of my wife's birthdays (when we were still engaged) where I had to go to her house. She is a twin. Her twin sister was engaged and her fiancé just came back from England that week. I already knew that I was very deep in the *comparison net*. I saw the gift he got for her, a very nice car. I went there on a bike and didn't even have the money to pay the bike man.

Vitória É Certa | Niyi Borire

The man had to wait for me to knock on the gate to get the bike fare from my wife. It wasn't easy for me. Whenever I was in their house, it was only my wife that stayed with me. I was not a fan.

Shockingly, as I entered their house this particular birthday, my wife's mum hugged me and said, *'Niyi, thank you for that beautiful gift'*. I was really surprised because the only gift I had on me was a powerful love letter (about four pages) I had written that morning (Remember that I mentioned earlier that I was an expert in this area). I knew that Olayemi loved my letters. Recently, we went on a date where she brought out all the letters. I couldn't believe it. We started reading the letters together. Back to the birthday story. What Olayemi did was that a week before her birthday, she had used all her savings to buy herself some very beautiful shoes. The previous year, it was a love letter she got from me while her twin sister got a lot of gifts from Dubai. So, this time around Olayemi stretched for my sake to cover up for me. I was so grateful. That day, I made up my mind that no matter what anyone thinks, I was going to marry her. She protected me and she didn't even tell me. That melted my heart.

Finances move people, but it didn't move her away from her conviction about me.

On our tenth wedding anniversary, we stayed in a suite in London where we could see Buckingham palace when we opened the window. It was like a palace itself. And I looked back at 15 years before when I would hop on a bike to my wife's house. Those days we will go out and she will have to pay because I had no money, all I had was my time and a very sweet mouth. All I needed was for her to understand me and believe in me, which she did. I assured her that we will get there. All I had was a conviction of where God was taking me and I had a lady who could see it with me and was ready to go all the way even though I wasn't spoiling her with money as some men will do. In the beginning, it may not look good but stay there. Don't let money move you away from your purpose.

4. **Fiction**: Fiction is something that is invented, untrue, and unproven. It's a myth. There is a lot of fiction out there in the world. Statements like, '*No man has ever done this*', '*This is impossible*', '*No black woman can have this kind of business in*

this area and succeed'. And these things can get into our head and prevent us from moving into our purpose. Don't allow such unproven truths to limit you.

5. **Fear**: Fear paralyses a man. Fear can move us away from our identity. Peter had walked and worked with Jesus for three years, however, when fear came, he was quick to change his identity; '*I don't know who you are talking about. I am not related to him*'. He denied Jesus because of fear. When people are afraid, they leave their purpose. You need to fight fear. Believe in yourself and conquer fear. Courage is not the absence of fear. Courage is standing your ground in the midst of fear. The courageous man is not the man that is not afraid. The courageous man is the one that can face his fears and overcome them. Don't let fear move you away. Elijah, who had previously called down fire from heaven to show the supremacy of God and had executed thousands of the prophets of Baal, ran away because of Jezebel's threat. Fear will make you reduce your worth.

Some of us are afraid to ask for or propose something that we desire because of fear. Go ahead and ask for the pay rise, favour, product, negotiation, etc. Ask! The worst thing that can happen is that you will get a no. This has helped me a lot personally. I am not afraid to ask or negotiate. I lay a demand.

6. **Facts**: Sometimes, statistics move us. People often throw facts into our face, '*It cannot be done*'. The man that often says it cannot be done will soon be interrupted by a man that does it. Some people are masters of statistics. Statistics usually keep a ceiling over us. There are a lot of things statistics tell us cannot happen because they have never happened before. For instance, the odds were against Leicester City to win the Premier League a few years ago but they went ahead to do it. You can always break the cycle.

At times, the vision God places in our hearts has no statistical backing. You cannot afford to live your life based on facts and stats. Your life should be lived based on your purpose and identity.

Vitória É Certa | Niyi Borire

How Can You Be Immovable?

'Therefore, my brethren, be ye steadfast, unmovable...' 1 Corinthians 15:58

The secret to being immovable is being steadfast. Steadfast is from two words, stead (which means a place) and fast (which means firmly fixed). So, you need to be firmly fixed in the place where God has put you. When you are firmly fixed where God has placed you, you will stand FAST.

Fixed: Fix your eyes on Jesus. Don't look at the storm.

Abound: Abound in God's work. Wherever God has placed you, do everything you can there. I remember a friend of mine when we were in medical school who was working as a security in the bank. He would often borrow our clothes (suits) and shoes to go attend parties around the school on Saturdays. He will discuss politics and drink wine but will trek a long distance. No one screened him at those parties because he was always well dressed. He eventually got a job in that same bank where he was a security guard because one day he told one of the notable people there that though he was a graduate he was working as a security guard. He was called, interviewed, and got the job. He is now an accomplished man. Whatever you are doing, give it your best.

Sail: Sail with other believers. Move with people that will encourage you. People who believe in the beauty of your dreams. People that will help you see that you are better than you think you are. Don't move with people that will drag you down. Move with people that will build you up, not the ones that will compete with you. Don't allow an inferiority complex either. Celebrate other people's success.

Trust: When God gives you a word, hold on to it and run with it. Believe what God has said. Run your race with that word He has given. It may be difficult but stay with that word.

2

POWER

When we talk of victory, it means there has been a challenge, battle, or war. You cannot be victorious over nothing. You cannot experience victory without having staying power. In life, we must realise that the enemy understands that we are already victorious by virtue of what Christ has done, however, he attacks us with weariness.

'And he shall speak great words against the most High, and shall wear out the saints of the most High, and think to change times and laws: and they shall be given into his hand until a time and times and the dividing of time'. (Daniel 7:25).

Also, he makes us feel that our problems are unique. There is no unique problem.

"There hath no temptation taken you but such as is common to man: but God is faithful, who will not suffer you to be tempted above that ye are able; but will with the temptation also make a way to escape, that ye may be able to bear it." (1 Corinthians 10:13)

The issue is not about receiving but if we will keep asking. *'Ask, and it shall be given you; seek, and ye shall find; knock, and it shall be opened unto you: For every one that asketh receiveth; and he that seeketh findeth; and to him that knocketh it shall be opened'.* (Mathew 7:7-8)

In our pursuit of victory through persistence in life, we must also be persistent in the place of prayer. *"And he spake a parable unto them to this end, that men ought always to pray, and not to faint;"* (Luke 18:1)

Reasons Why God Wants You To Pray

1. Prayer is God's method of achieving results in His kingdom.
2. Prayer is the channel of God's grace (Hebrews 4;16).
3. Prayer is the key that opens doors.
4. Prayer has no expiry date.
5. Prayer is the power of a Christian.

6. Prayer is exchanging man's weakness for God's strength (Isaiah 40:31).

Prayer Lessons From Bartimaeus

'And they came to Jericho: and as he went out of Jericho with his disciples and a great number of people, blind Bartimaeus, the son of Timaeus, sat by the highway side begging. And when he heard that it was Jesus of Nazareth, he began to cry out, and say, Jesus, thou Son of David, have mercy on me. And many charged him that he should hold his peace: but he cried the more a great deal, Thou Son of David, have mercy on me. And Jesus stood still, and commanded him to be called. And they call the blind man, saying unto him, Be of good comfort, rise; he calleth thee. And he, casting away his garment, rose, and came to Jesus. And Jesus answered and said unto him, What wilt thou that I should do unto thee? The blind man said unto him, Lord, that I might receive my sight. And Jesus said unto him, Go thy way; thy faith hath made thee whole. And immediately he received his sight, and followed Jesus in the way'. (Mark 10:46-52)

Bartimaeus was a man who had a challenge (blindness) and chose to call upon the name of God. The fact that we are born again doesn't preclude us from challenges or afflictions. Bartmaeus' challenge was that he was born blind. What did he do? At times, we go through difficult situations that force us to ask why we are going through them. Just like the man that was born blind in John 9:1-3, people are quick to ask who sinned because they attach challenges to sin. The reason we pass through challenges is for the glory of God to be seen.

Bartimaeus was begging on the road. From that scripture, Jesus was on his way out of that city towards the cross. Thus, Bartimaeus may have missed that opportunity forever if he didn't seize it. He did three things that helped him get his answers:

1. **He was positioned**: In life, positioning is very important. He sat by the roadside begging. He was where people could see him and he too could hear people passing by. He didn't go to the mall to beg. He was well-positioned to receive help.
2. **He was prepared**: He asked questions about Jesus that showed that he had done his research. He must have heard about Jesus to have believed that Jesus could help him. He didn't have eyes but his ears had heard about Jesus.
3. **He prayed**: Bartimaeus could have heard Jesus passing without getting healed. He cried out to

Jesus to have mercy on him. To pray is a legal term. He asked for mercy because God is merciful and mercy triumphs over judgement. Even though he was told to keep quiet by the people around Jesus, he refused to be silenced. He knew what he wanted. On our way to victory, men may try to silence us. On your way to what you want, you will be offered alternatives. Bartimaeus finally got an audience with Jesus, as soon as Jesus called him, he cast down his garment and ran towards Jesus. He had prayed, now he acted. Jesus asked him what he wanted and he asked that he may see. He didn't ask for a selfie or autograph. He received his sight just like he believed. He got what he demanded. Life doesn't give us what we deserve, it gives us what we demand. Whether the people around Jesus liked blind Bartimaeus or not, they made way for him to see Jesus.

OBTAINING VICTORY THROUGH POWER

The Christian is fighting a unique battle because Jesus has already won the victory on our behalf. In the spiritual realm, the devil is not impressed by your vocabulary. It is the knowledge you act on that gives you power. What the enemy respects is the anointing of God over your life. To live in power is to know God.

'Shall the prey be taken from the mighty, or the lawful captive delivered? But thus saith the LORD, Even the captives of the mighty shall be taken away, and the prey of the terrible shall be delivered: for I will contend with him that contendeth with thee, and I will save thy children'. (Isaiah 49:24-25). This scripture shows that certain situations are stronger and mightier than you which will require that you seek the help of a stronger power – God's. In the world, power is needed to get things done. What the enemy seeks to do is to prevent you from utilizing the power of God that is in you. *'For we wrestle not against flesh and blood, but against principalities, against powers, against the rulers of the darkness of this world, against spiritual wickedness in high places'.* (Ephesians 6:12) Failure to live as a representative of Christ by expressing the power of God that is resident in us, will strengthen the devil against us.

How to Obtain Power

The names of God that you know determines the power of God that you obtain or experience. This is because the names of God reflect the expressions of the power of God. Do you know Him as Jehovah Rapha so that you can experience His healing power in your life? Do you know Him as Jehovah Jireh, the Lord your provider? To know Him (Jesus) is to have power (John 14:9). To know Him is to know His ways. Do you know God's ways? To know His ways is to know His process. To know Him is to know His Word. To know Him is to know His Spirit.

The Cost of Power

We cannot isolate problems, challenges, from victory. In life, people go through battles and trials. One battle follows another. When you conquer one battle, another battle shows up. God has given us dominion (Genesis 1:28) but there can be no dominion without power. We need power to be victorious and we need victory to have dominion. Thus, we can conclude that the cost of power is more battles.

Why Do We Need to Be Empowered

1. **To exercise dominion**: Enemies submit to you because of power (Psalms 66:3)

2. **To have access to a power that is greater than the powers of the enemy**: One of the things we have seen in the church recently is that many believers say the devil has no power at all. In Luke 10:19, Jesus says that He has given us power over the power of the enemy.
3. **To fulfil our purpose or calling on the earth**: Without power, we can't fulfil our calling upon the earth. Jesus did nothing until He returned in the power of the Spirit (Luke 4:14, 18) Until He was empowered, He could not do the things He began to do. The Spirit of God upon Jesus turned Him into another man. He also told His disciples not to go out until they also received power (Luke 24:49) You go out without power, you get defeated.

As Christians, we must understand that we can't be who God has called us to be without power. The devil doesn't respect you because of what you have or have accomplished in life. The only thing he respects is power. Nothing of value in life is free. Even salvation caused God His Son and it cost Jesus His life. Victory is not cheap.

'And he rose up that night, and took his two wives, and his two womenservants, and his eleven sons, and passed

Vitória É Certa | Niyi Borire

over the ford Jabbok. And he took them, and sent them over the brook, and sent over that he had. And Jacob was left alone; and there wrestled a man with him until the breaking of the day. And when he saw that he prevailed not against him, he touched the hollow of his thigh; and the hollow of Jacob's thigh was out of joint, as he wrestled with him. And he said, Let me go, for the day breaketh. And he said, I will not let thee go, except thou bless me. And he said unto him, What is thy name? And he said, Jacob. And he said, Thy name shall be called no more Jacob, but Israel: for as a prince hast thou power with God and with men, and hast prevailed. And Jacob asked him, and said, Tell me, I pray thee, thy name. And he said, Wherefore is it that thou dost ask after my name? And he blessed him there. And Jacob called the name of the place Peniel: for I have seen God face to face, and my life is preserved. And as he passed over Penuel the sun rose upon him, and he halted upon his thigh. Therefore the children of Israel eat not of the sinew which shrank, which is upon the hollow of the thigh, unto this day: because he touched the hollow of Jacob's thigh in the sinew that shrank.'

In the passage above, we see that in order to prevail, the first power you need is power with God which will eventually translate to power with men. This kind of power that Jacob had cost him some things as follows:

1. **Discipline**: He sent everyone away to have some alone time with God.
2. **Desperation**: What you do not desire, you don't deserve. Jacob kept fighting because he was desperate. In Matthew 7:7-10, Jesus encourages us to be desperate in the pursuit of our desires in the place of prayer.
3. **Determination**: Jacob was determined to see that battle with the angel to the end. Despite his injury inflicted by the angel, he kept on fighting until his name was changed, and by extension his destiny.

STRENGTH FOR THE WEAK HANDS AND FEEBLE KNEES

'Wherefore lift up the hands which hang down, and the feeble knees' (Hebrews 12:12)

'Strengthen ye the weak hands, and confirm the feeble knees'. (Isaiah 35:3)

The word feeble in Hebrews is from the Greek word *paraleo* which means paralysed. If your knees are weak, you cannot stand and if you can't stand, you cannot walk.

Why Do We Get Weak Hands and Feeble Knees?

1. **Exertion**: As we exert ourselves doing what we should normally do, we become weak. You don't have to be sinning to experience feebleness
2. **Exhaustion**: The issues of life can exhaust us. We can become feeble because we are busy with many things. If we are not careful, our busyness will take us away from God.
3. **Erosion**: Our confidence can be eroded by the challenges around us. A lot of people give up because they lose their confidence. Many times, they give up too soon.
4. **Extraction**: Grace can be extracted from a man's life through sin and compromise. Sin should not be covered. The only way you deal with sin is by exposing it. Sin will keep leaking the grace of God out of your life. You cannot afford to tolerate sin in your life. Like Judas, you must not be comfortable operating in darkness even though you are close to the light.

How to Get Strength

1. **Evaluation**: Evaluate your present state, not your reputation or what people have to say about you. We have a cloud of witnesses watching us (Hebrews 12:1).
2. **Ejection**: Eject every weight and besetting sin. Put structures in place e.g. accountability.
3. **Expansion**: You need to expand your courage. Make up your mind to.
4. **Elevation**: Lift your eyes to God, because your help comes from Him.

GOD HAS NOT GIVEN US THE SPIRIT OF FEAR BUT THAT OF POWER

Fear is a natural occurrence. A primitive and powerful human emotion. Every one of us has been afraid before. It is okay to feel physical fear. Some people fear heights, water, etc. The worst kind of fear is the psychological one. The fear emotion is controlled by a part of the brain called the amygdala. The more we fear, the more our brains register it so much that we may interpret everything clothed in what our brains perceive as fear as something we should be afraid of. Fear can so cripple us that we worry ourselves about things that don't matter. Fear bloats things beyond what they are. For instance, you want to start a venture and you are already thinking about a million things that can go wrong. Psychological fear can cause social anxiety (you are afraid to gather with people), emotional disorders, etc.

Sometimes, we think it is okay to be afraid of physical dangers or failure but do you know that some people are afraid of success? They are so accustomed to being afraid that they now fear success. It is called *Achievemephobia*. It makes successful people self-destruct because, in their mindset, they believe that they are not meant to be there or they don't deserve it. There is another fear called *Atychiphobia* where someone believes that failure is part of their journey no matter what they do. These ones are so attached to failure in their mind that they do not even attempt to succeed.

Fear is a major obstacle to our victory in life because the devil can use something that has started in our minds against us. A lot of times, we try to do something but because we have experienced certain failures in the past, we don't even attempt to do that thing that should have been a walk in the pack for us.

Four Ways the Devil Uses Fear Against Us

1. **Deception**: In John 8:44, Jesus clearly stated that the devil is the father of lies. And one way he uses fear against us is to deceive us. He deceives us into thinking that our failures will keep repeating themselves, hence we don't push or try. We must never allow our failures to get into our minds. Some people have remained in abusive relationships because they feel they won't get someone better. Some others stay on jobs they shouldn't spend more than 3 months on because they are not confident they will get better befitting jobs.

2. **Division**: A house divided against itself cannot stand. The devil will use fear to cause division among brethren. We hurt but don't seek help from those who should help us. The fear of opening up to our fellow brothers and sisters keeps us broken and divided. Division leads to isolation which leads to destruction faster. It's easy to attack an isolated person (Ecclesiastes 4:9-12).

3. **Diversion**: The devil uses fear as a diversionary tactic. When you are afraid, two things happen; you either get distracted or want to turn back

from the real goal. Fear takes our attention away from our purpose or identity.
4. **Discourage**: When we fail a few times, the devil gets us to fixate on them so that we don't want to try anymore.

Ways of Overcoming Fear

"Be sober, be vigilant; because your adversary the devil, as a roaring lion, walketh about, seeking whom he may devour: Whom resist steadfast in the faith, knowing that the same afflictions are accomplished in your brethren that are in the world." (1 Peter 5:8-9)

This scripture shows us what we need to do to overcome our fears. Let's highlight the main points:
1. **Sobriety**: In the midst of fear, we could panic and lose control. When we are sober and vigilant, we can see the devil for who he is and resist him.
2. **Situational Awareness**: We are in a battle. The devil is our adversary. If you understand this, it helps you to stay firm.
3. **Self-Awareness**: Be sure of who you are in Christ.
4. **Steadfastness**: You need to stand firm in God to be able to resist the devil.

IMPOSSIBILITY

To fight for something, you've got to understand what you are fighting for. You cannot be engaged in a battle when you don't know the worth that is at stake. You can't fight in a war when you don't know what the task is and how important it is. You must have watched war films where young guys or ladies (like 16 -18 years of age) go to war. It's because they understood that the salvation or safety of their countries rested on them. They didn't care about their lives because they had a bigger picture in mind. When you understand the importance of a course, you will be able to stretch yourself as far as you can go to fight for it. Esther (in Esther 4) was ready to sacrifice her life because she realised that the freedom of the Jews was resting on her. You have to understand the meaning of impossible in order for you to be engaged in the battle for the impossible. What is at stake?

'And a certain ruler asked him, saying, Good Master, what shall I do to inherit eternal life? And Jesus said unto him, Why callest thou me good? none is good, save one, that is, God. Thou knowest the commandments, Do not commit adultery, Do not kill, Do not steal, Do not bear false witness, Honour thy father and thy mother. And he said, All these have I kept from my youth

Vitória É Certa | Niyi Borire

up. Now when Jesus heard these things, he said unto him, Yet lackest thou one thing: sell all that thou hast, and distribute unto the poor, and thou shalt have treasure in heaven: and come, follow me. And when he heard this, he was very sorrowful: for he was very rich. And when Jesus saw that he was very sorrowful, he said, How hardly shall they that have riches enter into the kingdom of God! For it is easier for a camel to go through a needle's eye, than for a rich man to enter into the kingdom of God. And they that heard it said, Who then can be saved? And he said, The things which are impossible with men are possible with God.' (Luke 18:18-27)

The phrase, *The things which are impossible* in verse 27 is taken from the Greek word *Adunatus* which means impotent, powerless, weak, or disabled. What Jesus meant here is that what makes the situation impossible is not the situation itself but the weakness of the man in the situation. I remember when we were in school, after an exam in medical school, you would find students consulting each other to find out what the correct answer to a certain question was. Some will consider the exam tough, others will consider it simple. That means what is impossible for one person is possible for another. The difference is not the level of difficulty of the exam but the level of the inherent strengths of the students.

Therefore, when Jesus looked at the rich man, he knew that rich men could enter heaven because of righteous men like Abraham, Solomon, etc. who have been rich in the past. Hence, the problem is not the level of your difficulty or how big your mountain is, the problem is how small your faith and strength are. So, in that scripture, Jesus wasn't referring to powerless things but powerless men. However, when you come to the Lord's side all things are possible. The word possible there is from the Greek word *Dunatus* a variation of *Dunamis* which means power. This refers to the power of God to make things happen. So, it's not the impossible situation but the impossible, powerless, weak, or faithless man. Impossible doesn't describe the situation but the person; the impotent man, faithless man, powerless man. Impossible doesn't necessarily;

- express the difficulty or complexity of a task. When you say, *I can't carry out the assignment or task, it is impossible*; it's because you feel weak, faithless, intimidated, or incapable.
- reflect the vastness and bulkiness of the obstacle. When Jesus used the word impossible, He wasn't

talking about the greatness, vastness, bulkiness of the obstacle.
- reflect the horror or terror of the situation.
- reflect the severity or gravity of the pain.

None of the above reflects impossibility. The man who says it is impossible will soon be overtaken by the man who does it.

The Impossible Man

The word impossible does three things:

1. **It defines a man**: when you put the word impossible before a man, it defines him. When you use the word impossible, you define yourself by the situation. The account in Numbers 13:25-33 explains this well:

'And they returned from searching of the land after forty days. And they went and came to Moses, and to Aaron, and to all the congregation of the children of Israel, unto the wilderness of Paran, to Kadesh; and brought back word unto them, and unto all the congregation, and shewed them the fruit of the land. And they told him, and said, We came unto the land whither thou sentest us, and surely it floweth with milk and honey; and this is the fruit of it. Nevertheless the people be strong that dwell in the

land, and the cities are walled, and very great: and moreover we saw the children of Anak there. The Amalekites dwell in the land of the south: and the Hittites, and the Jebusites, and the Amorites, dwell in the mountains: and the Canaanites dwell by the sea, and by the coast of Jordan.

And Caleb stilled the people before Moses, and said, Let us go up at once, and possess it; for we are well able to overcome it. But the men that went up with him said, We be not able to go up against the people; for they are stronger than we. And they brought up an evil report of the land which they had searched unto the children of Israel, saying, The land, through which we have gone to search it, is a land that eateth up the inhabitants thereof; and all the people that we saw in it are men of a great stature. And there we saw the giants, the sons of Anak, which come of the giants: and we were in our own sight as grasshoppers, and so we were in their sight.'

These men returned from searching the land after forty days. Their conclusion of that search was that they were powerless. They defined themselves as small, and like grasshoppers, not only in their sight but also in the sight of the people of the land. Maybe they came to that conclusion because they were spies (undercovers). How did they know that the people they have not interacted with saw them as grasshoppers? The problem is that we ascribe our perception of ourselves to others.

2. **It describes a man**: When you use the word impossible, you describe your value or worth. Acts 14:8 says, '*There sat a certain man at Lystra who was impotent in his feet, being a cripple from his mother's womb, who never had walked:*' The word impossible describes the powerlessness of a man.

3. **It decides a man**: When you put impossible before a man's name, you have decided his fate. You have given up already. It has decided his future. '*If thou faint in the day of adversity, thy strength is small*' (Proverbs 24:10). The faint here doesn't mean collapsing, it is referring to being inactive or doing nothing. Your strength is small because you didn't try. I remember one UFC highlight I saw recently where one of the fighters tapped out the moment he saw the size of his opponent. He concluded that he had no chance and was going to lose anyway. So, instead of being battered by his opponent's punches, he quickly tapped to accept defeat without even trying. When you faint, you don't even try at all, you just give up. You turn back when you see the size of your opposition.

The Possible God

'Hast thou not known? Hast thou not heard, that the everlasting God, the LORD, the Creator of the ends of the earth fainteth not, neither is weary. There is no searching out of his understanding.' (Isaiah 40:28). We have seen the definition of fainting earlier. Weary means you tried but got exhausted. It means giving up. A faint man cannot start the battle, while a weary man cannot finish the battle. A weary man is exhausted by toiling. He cannot finish well. *'He giveth power to the faint; and to them that have no might he increaseth strength.'* (Isaiah 40:29)

Can you observe the dynamics in the scripture above? One would have thought that it should read as, *to him who has no might, he giveth power* but it says that he increases strength meaning there was strength before, it only gets multiplied. As far as God is concerned, the man that says he has no might may have little strength but as he waits on God, God multiplies his strength so much that he becomes powerful and that situation that has been termed impossible becomes possible because he waited on God.

'Even the youths shall faint and be weary, and the young men shall utterly fall; but they that wait on the LORD shall renew their strength, they shall mount up with wings

Vitória É Certa | Niyi Borire

like eagles. They shall run and not be weary, they shall walk and not faint.' (Isaiah 40:30-31). God is a specialist in renewing strength and bringing possibility out of impossibility.

3
PASSION

Every child of God must desire to know more of God. That should be their heart cry. A cry that wants to experience more of God. When this desire starts to wane, such a person is drawing away from God. Sometimes, when we get encumbered with a lot of activities, this cry begins to die. From the scripture below, we see that David wasn't satisfied with where he was. He wanted more of God. The worst place to be is where you have become familiar with the workings of God. The greatest damage that can happen to a man is to assume that he has seen all of God.

'O God, thou art my God; early will I seek thee: my soul thirsteth for thee, my flesh longeth for thee in a dry and thirsty land, where no water is; To see thy power and thy glory, so as I have seen thee in the sanctuary. Because

Vitória É Certa | Niyi Borire

thy lovingkindness is better than life, my lips shall praise thee. Thus will I bless thee while I live: I will lift up my hands in thy name. My soul shall be satisfied as with marrow and fatness; and my mouth shall praise thee with joyful lips: When I remember thee upon my bed, and meditate on thee in the night watches. Because thou hast been my help, therefore in the shadow of thy wings will I rejoice. My soul followeth hard after thee: thy right hand upholdeth me.' (Psalms 63:1-8)

We cannot fully understand God. There is no way we can fully explore Him. Self-satisfaction is a form of self-deception. I remember the story of a guy who travelled overseas and was so excited when he saw a skyscraper. In excitement, he started counting the storeys of the skyscraper. A scammer, who saw it as an opportunity to take advantage, spotted the guy from a distance, walked up to him, and told him that it was unlawful to be counting the number of storeys in a skyscraper. So, the scammer asked the guy how many storeys he had counted. He said 10 whereas he had counted 20. So, the scammer charged the guy a fine of 1 USD per level which the guy paid. When the scammer left, the guy started laughing because he felt he had cheated the scammer by paying 10 USD when he should have paid 20 USD. Who was scammed in the scenario?

Certainly, it was the guy who was counting the storeys that was scammed. He was scammed, yet he thought he had cheated the scammer.

It's possible for you to have an experience of God and you assume that you have arrived. That is self-deception. If you know how much of God you can experience, you will be ashamed of where you are at the moment. I believe some of us will be surprised when we get to heaven only to realise that we only scratched the surface of God's potential. In heaven, some of us will have regrets like, '*Oh, I didn't explore more, I didn't give more because of work and family.*'

I can't forget a movie I watched, *Schindler's List*, about the genocide of the Jews. Schindler, a Jew, wasn't a good man in the movie but he was making pots and pantries for the German Soldiers. He figured that the best way to make money was to cut costs, so he went to the Jewish camp where Jews were imprisoned. There were some educated Jews there, and he requested for them to join him to make pots and pans for him at no salary in his factory. He provided them protection and food even though he wasn't paying them a salary. As the war progressed, his conscience began to prick him. He saw how Jews were being killed in the camps. When the war ended, he came to the factory to announce that the war was over, and all of them were crying, holding on to him, thanking him for sparing their lives. He left the factory and as he drove away in his car, he was crying because he felt that he could have done more when he realised that 3-4 million Jews were killed in the town where he was. Even though he was praised, he knew he could have done a bit more.

More of God means you have experienced a bit of God. You can't want more of something that you have not tasted a little of. If you have had an encounter or experience with God, then I challenge you to go for more. I hope that you don't get to that point where you wish you could have done more. A time comes when, even if you want to do more, there will be no more time or energy to get it done.

The Characteristics of the Cry for More of God

1. **It is a personal cry**: The pursuit of God is personal (like we saw in Psalms 63:1). God works through personal revelation and encounters. If you want to experience more of God, you must pursue Him personally. You must deliberately follow hard after Him. '*As the hart pants after the*

water brooks, so my soul longs after you.' (Psalms 42:1)

2. **It is passionate**: Psalms 84:2 says, *'My soul longeth, yea even fainteth for the courts of the LORD: my heart and my flesh crieth out for the living God.'* If you want more of God, you have to give Him more of you. It is a tripartite pursuit – spirit, soul, and body. You have to be passionate about pursuing God.

3. **It is pertinent**: This means something important or relevant. God's right hand will uphold you when you pursue Him diligently (Psalms 63:8). Pursuing God is pertinent to your breakthrough. When you pursue Him diligently, every other thing will fall in place. God rewards those who diligently seek Him (Hebrews 11:6). No one pursues God and ever regrets. He will take care of you and answer your prayers. The key to sustainable victory is not in prayers and fastings but in pursuing God genuinely and diligently. There is a lot of favour you will enjoy and needs that will be met when you seek after God. When you seek after God, all other things will be added unto you (Mathew 6:33) God won't come chasing after you, you have to want Him and

chase Him. God has a lot more in store for you than what you are presently enjoying.
4. **It is practical**: A cry is practical, not theoretical. It is realistic.

Three Ways You Can Pursue and Enjoy More of God

1. **Through Prayers**: Psalms 63:1 says, '*Oh lord thou art my God, early will I seek thee...*' You've got to seek God. The secret to seeking God is not in the duration but the frequency. The consistency and frequency matter the most. There is the story of a man named Jack who goes to the chapel every day and all he says daily is, '*Oh Lord God, this is Jack checking. I love you. Please help me*'. That was his daily routine until the priest of the chapel noticed that Jack wasn't showing up anymore. So, the priest went in search of Jack. The priest went to the factory where Jack was working and he found out that Jack had been sick for a while. The priest located the hospital Jack was in and noticed that he was all by himself, no flowers, letters, or anyone with him. The priest told Jack that he just came to check on him because he noticed that Jack always showed up by

noon to pray every day and suddenly didn't show up anymore.

The priest went on to express his concern for Jack who he believed must have been very lonely since there was nothing around him that showed that he had people caring for him. Jack replied that his stay in the hospital has been his best days on earth because at noon every day, a man walks in to say, *'Hi Jack, it's me Jesus, I just came to check on you to see that you are fine'*. Jack told the priest that that was enough for him. God values your consistency in little things. What is the essence of going on a 3 days marathon fasting and prayer when you don't pray for the remainder of the year?

2. **Through the Word**: To pursue God, you have to be hungry for His Word. God's Word has purity in itself and gives insight. You must give yourself to God's Word because that is how He reveals Himself to us.

FORGETTING THE PAST

'Not as though I had already attained, either were already perfect: but I follow after, if that I may apprehend that for which also I am apprehended of Christ

Jesus. Brethren, I count not myself to have apprehended: but this one thing I do, forgetting those things which are behind, and reaching forth unto those things which are before, I press toward the mark for the prize of the high calling of God in Christ Jesus. Let us therefore, as many as be perfect, be thus minded: and if in any thing ye be otherwise minded, God shall reveal even this unto you.' (Philippians 3:12-15)

Paul, through these verses, is acknowledging that he was on a journey of transformation. If you are going to be who God has designed you to be or get what He has prepared for you to enjoy, then there are many things that you must forget. You cannot make progress in certain areas of your life if you don't forget some things from the past.

I realised that the reason why some of us are not where God wants us to be or enjoying what He has prepared for us to enjoy is that we are not forgetting the things we ought to forget. This is the one time that you are allowed to have memory loss. You can't press forward if you don't forget certain things. How can you press when you are still holding on to the past?

God cannot be fully explored by holding on to a single experience. Why don't you have your breakfast, lunch, and dinner together and say you have filled yourself for the whole day? It's because no matter what you eat, your body will break it down. The food will expire as it were and you will need another food experience. So, if on a normal day you have to eat three times to get the required energy levels and stay healthy, one-time eating (no matter the quantity or quality cannot sustain you. In like manner, how can we depend on a single experience of God to get all of God? You cannot experience all of God in a day or meeting. You have to keep experiencing God. You have to keep pressing. You have to keep searching. You have to keep exposing yourself. There are portals in God that are yet to be opened by any man. There is more of God to learn, explore, and experience. You shouldn't be satisfied with where you are, you need to press forward. To press forward, however, there are things we need to forget:

1. **Forget your past mistakes**: One of the things that can hold you down from experiencing more of God is your past mistakes. The devil can use that to hold you but God will never condemn you. There is no condemnation for those who are in Christ Jesus (Romans 8:1-2) When you come into union with Christ, the condemnation of sin is gone. You can't live under it anymore. It doesn't matter how horrible your past was, you cannot tie yourself to the mistakes of the past because you won't be able to move forward. A lot

of people can't press into more of God because they are tied to their pasts. We all make mistakes in life but we can't afford to be held down by them. Stand up and move on. The glory of Christianity is not in never falling but in rising every time we fall. You can arise! The beauty of our experience with God is that we rise. Put the past behind you. It doesn't matter what people have said about you or think about you, the past is the past. You can make up your mind to live a life that counts for God.

2. **Forget the past medals**: Forget the past achievements. If you want to achieve more, you have to forget your past achievements. Sometimes, the enemy of the best is good. You need to forget some of your good experiences so you can reach for more. To get more of God, you need to crave a new experience. You can't live on yesterday's anointing or experience. Yesterday's anointing cannot take care of today's challenges. It may keep you busy or give you a form of godliness but it won't move you into the new that God has in store for you.

3. **Forget the past manna**: Manna here refers to the Word. When was the last time God spoke to you? Do you even know God personally? Or are

you just playing church? You have to feed on God's Word. That's the way to know Him. You can get more intimate with Him. There is something better and bigger. Desire something deeper with God. It may require your sacrifice but give it what it takes. It always pays off in the end.

I remember that when I finished my training as a specialist, I had the opportunity to just work in a small hospital and be put on a consultant salary but I wanted something more than that. It wasn't common in my field for someone to finish training as a specialist and then enroll in a university as a full-time student but I did. I enrolled for my Ph.D. and was earning a 35,000 USD stipend then. It was way below what I was earning while training as a specialist but I knew that I had to sacrifice. I had to go low to get high and God opened up other doors for me to fill in the gaps.   Without that sacrifice, I won't be working in a teaching hospital now.

When I first got to Australia, the first contract job offer I got was to be a GP (General Practitioner) in a town of 600 people which would earn me 180, 000 USD pay, 5 Bedroom Apartment with no bills. That was not what I wanted. I signed the contract but didn't take the job eventually. Rather, I settled for a 55, 000 USD job, no house (I was squatting with a Pakistani guy who almost killed me with his curry), in cold, no car, but I knew what I wanted. I knew there was something better ahead. Sometimes, you may need to go low first. You may need to go back to school after achieving what others will call a great feat, don't hesitate to.

Recently, my wife had to apply to enroll for a law degree. Four years time, she will be a practicing solicitor in Australia. When we first got here, she wanted to be a lawyer but we couldn't afford it. She had to settle for nursing because we wanted her to train in something that can get her a job anywhere in Australia. She had to study Science courses that she had no background in. That year, she got a distinction in Science. She finished with a Bachelor's degree (gave birth to our two children during this period) and went ahead to do her master's to be a specialist stroke nurse. This was her third degree but she isn't giving up yet.

For 12 months we had been discussing her returning to school to study law which has finally happened. It has taken 11 years for that dream (of studying law) to be realised. She reminds me of the fact that our journeys are different in life. God will sometimes take us through a detour but He knows where He is taking us. Hence, you must not settle for less. You have to push yourself and do what you have to do. You may be 40 or 50 but if you know that you need to go back to school, then go for it. Don't compare yourself with others. Forget your past achievements.

4. **Forget the past methods**: Be flexible. Be sensitive to the Spirit. The way it worked 10 years ago may not be how it will work now. The way it worked for someone else may not be how it will work for you. There is no formula for everything. I know of a friend who courted his wife for just three months, and they are enjoying their marriage. Someone else may try that and regret it for the rest of his life. Our journeys are different. For you, it may require 6 years of courtship. Forget the past methods. Be open to the new.

4

PURITY

The Psalmist makes an important enquiry, '*Who shall ascend into the hill of the LORD? or who shall stand in his holy place? He that hath clean hands, and a pure heart; who hath not lifted up his soul unto vanity, nor sworn deceitfully. He shall receive the blessing from the LORD, and righteousness from the God of his salvation. This is the generation of them that seek him, that seek thy face, O Jacob. Selah.*' (Psalms 24:3-6)

The hill of the Lord here may refer to heaven, the earth, or the presence of God. The question is answered from verse 4, '*He that hath clean hands...*' The first requirement is **clean hands**. Your hand is a visible part of you when compared to your heart that can't be seen physically. Hence, what this is communicating is that the outward, visible, palpable part of you must be clean. Why is the answer starting with the external? It's because it is important. I know people who say things like it is the heart that matters, it really doesn't matter what I do with my body.

Well, it is indeed the heart that matters but you can't have a pure heart with unclean hands. It just doesn't make sense. Yet, this is what some people want us to believe. That they may drink alcohol, womanise, smoke, etc. and it doesn't matter as long as their hearts are right. That can't be correct. People will see your exterior first. When the Bible says in Matthew 5:16 that *'Let your light so shine before men that they may see your good works and glorify your father in heaven'*, it is talking about your exterior because that is what people will see and identify with, hence it must be clean. Your external life must be attractive and compelling.

The next requirement from that scripture is a **pure heart**. This talks about inward purity. A true conscience. And it is as important as clean hands. Is it possible to have clean hands without a pure heart? Absolutely! It is possible to be morally upright without having that deep walk of faith in your heart. It is possible to have an appearance of godliness but deny the power thereof. It is even possible to be in the church and work for God and still not have a deep connection with Christ. Externally you look okay but deep down, you are something else. Christianity is who you are behind closed doors. It is easy to behave well among fellow Christians.

The third requirement is a focused mind. The man who has not lifted up his soul unto vanity. The last requirement is **rough knees** which refer to prayer. The generation of them that seek God. *'Nevertheless, the foundation of God standeth sure, having this seal, The Lord knoweth them that are his...'* (2 Timothy 2:19, 21-22). Those who belong to God are those who have departed from sin. The church is not only for social interaction or feeling good. If you want to be God's you cannot be soiled. You cannot perpetually live in compromise and still be God's. Purity is a process that God Himself initiates in your heart. However, you have a role to play by departing from iniquity. It is your responsibility to flee youthful lusts. You can't have a pure heart without fleeing youthful lusts.

How Can You Have Purity?

The word purity is from the root word PURE. To understand purity, I have used the acronym PURE to explain below:

1. **Pursue**: There can be no purity without pursuit. You cannot live a pure life if you do not pursue it. You can't be pure by accident, you need to be determined. Pursuit is achieved through hunger or desire. Pursuit is not easy. You don't turn back until you have gotten what you are chasing after. I have been pursued before. I remember going to see a patient after work one day. I was called by a woman whose daughter was sick. I entered their compound and got to their door. I knocked and the mother opened the door but unknown to her, their dog walked past her and started pursuing me. It was a very big dog whose big face looked more to me like a lion.

    All I saw on its face was a desire to hurt me, so I ran for my dear life. My only desire was to live, so all the tiredness flew away. I had a briefcase in my hand but it didn't stop me from running. Funnily, my driver, who also feared dogs, just took off with the car the moment he saw that I was being chased by a dog. So funny. I never went to that house again. The woman called me to apologise and still wanted me to come but I told her that it wasn't possible. I asked her to go look for another doctor.

'Blessed are they who hunger and thirst for righteousness for they shall be filled' (Matthew 5:6). We cannot have purity without being thirsty or hungry for it. To live a pure life, you've got to be determined. Do you think if a lady was trying to seduce me that day I was running for my life I would have waited? No way! God's standard is sure. Without holiness, you can't make heaven. Purity is not optional. If you live in perpetual sin, you are on your way to hell no matter what you are doing for God.

2. **Undo**: To undo is to cancel or to reverse the effects or result of a previous action. For instance, you may want to type *'I am a woman'* on your word document on the computer, and you mistakenly type, *'I am a man'*. You don't go ahead to type the correct thing after you have written the wrong thing as that will confuse the reader, who will think you are saying that you are both a man and a woman. What you do, instead, is to undo the wrong statement. That's more like reversing what was done initially.

It is not possible to build your spirituality on a lifestyle of sin. If there is impurity in your life, it has to be undone first. It has to be taken away. Otherwise, you are building your house on shaky ground that will not stand. The foundation of true anointing or ministry is consecration. Samson built his ministry on a shaky foundation of fornication and it finally crumbled.

'This I say therefore, and testify in the Lord, that ye henceforth walk not as other Gentiles walk, in the vanity of their mind, Having the understanding darkened, being alienated from the life of God through the ignorance that is in them, because of the blindness of their heart: Who being past feeling have given themselves over unto lasciviousness, to work all uncleanness with greediness. But ye have not so learned Christ; If so be that ye have heard him, and have been taught by him, as the truth is in Jesus: That ye put off concerning the former conversation the old man, which is corrupt according to the deceitful lusts; And be renewed in the spirit of your mind; And that ye put on the new man, which after God is created in righteousness and true holiness.

Wherefore putting away lying, speak every man truth with his neighbour: for we are members one of another. Be ye angry, and sin not: let not the sun go down upon your wrath: Neither give place to the devil. Let him that stole steal no more: but rather let him labour, working with his hands the thing which is good, that he may have to give to him that needeth. Let no corrupt communication proceed out of your mouth, but that which is good to the use of edifying, that it may minister grace unto the hearers. And grieve not the holy Spirit of God, whereby ye are sealed unto the day of redemption. Let all bitterness, and wrath, and anger, and clamour, and evil speaking, be put away from you, with all malice: And be ye kind one to another, tenderhearted, forgiving one another, even as God for Christ's sake hath forgiven you.' (Ephesians 4:17-32)

Here, the scripture (which was written to Christians) clearly warns against certain things that must not be found in a believer like lying, anger, stealing, etc. We are commanded to put off (undo) these things. It is our responsibility to put off these things even though we will rely on God's grace. (Hebrews 12:2) Don't put yourself in compromising situations.

3. **Review**: The best examination is self-examination (1 Corinthians 11:32) This is only possible if you have insight and sincerity. Insight simply refers to the ability to know that something is wrong. When you are sick and you don't know it, you lack insight. You can't examine yourself thoroughly if you don't have insight. Revelations 3:17 talks about the Ladoecian Christians who thought they were rich but were actually poor. Sincerity means accepting reality. That is, when you know that you are sick and accept that you are.

4. **Endue**: This is to be endowed with power and grace. This is achieved through the Word of God and prayer. (John 15:3, Psalms 119:5). The Word of God purifies us. When I was struggling with a besetting sin, I had to memorise the whole of Romans 6. Allow the Word of God to sink into you. David prayed to God concerning his purity (Psalms 51:1).

Finally, to stay pure, you need to WATCH. Watch your:

- **Words**: What you say is what you attract. Your words can be used against you. Your words must be seasoned to minister grace to the hearers. There is creative power in our words as believers, hence the need to watch what we say.
- **Actions**: These are reflective of our decision-making. They inform our routines. Our daily actions will either make or mar us. The seeming little activities we engage in daily can greatly influence the outcomes of our lives.
- **Thoughts**: Your thoughts make you. Your thoughts are powerful. Our thoughts create the environment in which our actions are carried out. Our thoughts could be spontaneous, that is, they pop up from sensory experiences. However, there are also intentional thoughts that are internally and consciously generated. Imaginations are visual thoughts. Thoughts can prime us for positive or negative behaviours.
- **Character**: Character is formed from repetitive actions. It also reflects our attitude to things. It's an external manifestation of your internal state of mind. It also connotes stability.
- **Habits**: We are all products of habits. Our habits eventually make us. They are formed by actions.

To watch our habits, then we must watch our actions.

REGARDLESS

The word regardless is taken from the word regard which means paying attention to something, having concern for something. So, regardless means not paying attention or not being concerned about something. What are those things in our lives that we should not pay attention to or be concerned about? What are those things that, though they are present, we shouldn't allow to control our reaction or decision-making?

We are meant to look away from those things that try to discourage us, scare us, mislead us, or turn our attention away from God. So many people have asked me why God allowed the COVID-19 pandemic to ravage the world. Sometimes, situations and circumstances happen that we can't really explain. God has not promised us a smooth life or life without challenges, what He has promised us is that even though we walk through the valley of the shadow of death, He will be with us. He has assured us to stand by us and see us through.

You need to understand that God is more than the prevailing circumstances that are presently weighing you down or challenging you. Apart from demanding our time and attention, these circumstances also feed our anxiety and worry. I know people who have chronic illnesses like migraine who keep worrying about it and as a result, it gets worse. So, what focusing on problems does is that the problem becomes bigger. Have you observed that a mountain becomes bigger as you move closer to it and smaller as you move farther away from it?

Regardless of the circumstances around you, you need to know that:

1. God loves you: No matter where you are or what you have done, Jesus loves you and this was proven by His laying down His life for your sake (John 15:13). Jesus loves you beyond your situation, pain, or sin (Romans 5:8)
2. You've got to give thanks: In every situation, give thanks (1 Thessalonians 5:18)

If it is sin that is holding you down or back, Jesus can save you (Isaiah 1:18). Jesus loves you the way you are. Even if your sin is so terrible, Jesus is willing to wash you and make you clean again. Don't dwell in your sin. Allow Jesus to clean you up.

If it is sickness that is weighing you down, there is healing available for you (3 John 3:2, Isaiah 53:5)

It may be a certain situation or circumstance that is holding you down. The lines are falling unto you in pleasant places (Psalms 16:6). Maybe you just lost your job, God is able to restore you.

It may be a stronghold in your mind, family, etc. that is holding you down, it is coming down by the power in the name of Jesus (2 Corinthians 10:5).

Maybe you have been afflicted by the devil and his spirits, Satan and his works in your life will fall (Luke 10:18) No generational curse can operate in your life. No negative pronouncement or declaration over your life will stand as long as you belong to God (Numbers 23:23).

5

PEACE

Let us begin with an interesting account. '*The first day of the week cometh Mary Magdalene early, when it was yet dark, unto the sepulchre, and seeth the stone taken away from the sepulchre. Then she runneth, and cometh to Simon Peter, and to the other disciple, whom Jesus loved, and saith unto them, They have taken away the Lord out of the sepulchre, and we know not where they have laid him. Peter therefore went forth, and that other disciple, and came to the sepulchre. So they ran both together: and the other disciple did outrun Peter, and came first to the sepulchre. And he stooping down, and looking in, saw the linen clothes lying; yet went he not in.*

Then cometh Simon Peter following him, and went into the sepulchre, and seeth the linen clothes lie, And the napkin, that was about his head, not lying with the linen clothes, but wrapped together in a place by itself. Then went in also that other disciple, which came first to the sepulchre, and he saw, and believed. For as yet they knew not the scripture, that he must rise again from the dead. Then the disciples went away again unto their own home. But Mary stood without at the sepulchre weeping: and as she wept, she stooped down, and looked into the sepulchre,' (John 20:1-11)

The first thing that caught my attention in the passage above was why Mary was crying at the Lord's grave. Mary had seen the empty grave first and ran to tell the other disciples to see what she had seen. They confirmed that, indeed, their Master was no longer there. The other disciples left afterwards, leaving her behind with the empty tomb. Is that not how you search for your Peter and John in life only for them to leave you without any encouragement?

The second question that came to my mind was why Mary was more concerned about Jesus' body than the disciples. Peter quickly returned to his fishing business but Mary stayed at the empty grave of Jesus. What was her problem? What was she doing at the grave on a Sunday morning? Didn't she have a husband?

Vitória É Certa | Niyi Borire

Let's look at the background story in Luke 8:1-3, '*And it came to pass afterward, that he went throughout every city and village, preaching and shewing the glad tidings of the kingdom of God: and the twelve were with him, And certain women, which had been healed of evil spirits and infirmities, Mary called Magdalene, out of whom went seven devils, And Joanna the wife of Chuza Herod's steward, and Susanna, and many others, which ministered unto him of their substance.*' Mary was once possessed by seven demons. She was wealthy but possessed. Money wasn't her problem. We never heard about her husband or children. There was something that wasn't right about her life until she met Jesus.

Jesus took a woman who was possessed and turned her life around. She became so prominent in Jesus' ministry that Matthew, Mark, Luke, and John all mentioned her name. She became so relevant that her name appeared more in scripture than some other disciples of Jesus. The first person to see the resurrected Jesus was this once demon-possessed, condemned woman. This realisation brought tears to my eyes. Jesus never gives up on anyone.

So, we can better relate to why Mary was so touched by Jesus' missing body. When all the apostles could not help her, she stayed there. When the angels appeared to her to ask why she was crying, she said, *'because they have taken away my Lord.'* She was looking for something so special to her. She was looking for her essence, her identity, the man who defines her. Even the angels couldn't give her an answer. She finally turned and saw Jesus but didn't immediately realise that it was Him. Like many times when Jesus is right there beside us in the midst of the storm or challenge but we don't recognise that He is the one. Jesus was there all the while but none of them saw Him.

If only your eyes will see Jesus in the midst of that storm. He is the source of your peace. Jesus asked Mary what the problem was. She still didn't realise He was the one. To know is to see Him. Peace comes from seeing Him. Mary assumed that Jesus was a gardener. He was different. He didn't look like the Jesus she used to know. Eventually, Jesus called her one more time and she turned in recognition. She now knew the voice, *Rabboni* she answered. She experienced peace immediately.

Jesus knew her pain, agony, past, and called her. She turned and saw. She had a revelation of peace. After that experience, Mary went to tell the other disciples about her revelation. Jesus finally showed up where His disciples were gathered and the first word He uttered was, *'Peace be unto you'*

PEACEMAKERS

'Blessed are the peacemakers: for they shall be called the children of God' (Matthew 5:9)

'Follow peace with all men and holiness, without which no man shall see the Lord' (Hebrews 12:14)

Here, we are referring to peace among men. Generally, everyone wants peace but not everyone is willing to do the work. Peacemaking requires action. It is not passive. To make something means to create, put together, bridge, or connect.

Peacemaking doesn't mean saying yes to everything. At times, to establish peace means saying no. Peacemaking doesn't require you to sacrifice your salvation either. Peacemaking doesn't mean everybody must agree with you. Peacemaking is not about control or shutting other people down. Peace is first pure (James 3:17)

You can't call yourself a child of God if you are not a peacemaker. It requires intentional pursuit. You have to seek and pursue peace. Peacemakers are people who can cooperate and show others how to cooperate rather than compete. Peace doesn't happen by chance. It must be worked upon. We are not just to be makers of peace, we should also be maintainers of peace. If it is not continuous, you are not yet a peacemaker. Peacemakers pursue peace consistently.

What Do Peacemakers Do?

1. Intentional forgiveness and reconciliation: You cannot have bitterness in your heart and pursue peace at the same time. Peace is meant to flow from your heart and bitterness will block that flow.
2. Common-unity: Our diversity is one of the things God has given us. We can work for the common good. A peacemaker bears with others in love. As humans, we are designed for community, not isolation. As far as it depends on you, live peaceably with all. If there is no peace in your community, you can't have peace.
3. Goodwill and kindness: We must sow peace with the words of our mouth. Sometimes, we can be right but our communication of it may be wrong. You need to improve your communication skills to pursue peace.
4. Humility: A peacemaker is always humble.

You cannot give peace if you don't have peace. You must make room for peace in your heart before you can dispense it to others. Above all, to have or share peace, you must know God. Peace brings clarity. So, wherever you are, pursue peace. As long as it lies with you, give room for peace.

PEACE IN THE STORM

Storms are inevitable. There is no man or woman who will not go through storms. Storms are a common denominator in our lives. What makes you human are the storms you go through, otherwise you will be an angel or God. The fact that you go through challenges and difficulties gives you the legal right to be human. It doesn't matter what you own, what you dream of owning, or what you aspire to be. Everybody will face storms in their life.

What is a storm? A storm is a violent disturbance or turbulence. I remember once when I was in business class flying to the United States and we faced turbulence. At that moment when the plane was moving up and down, it didn't matter what class we were flying, everyone had to sit up. It was the worst international flight I had ever been on. At that moment I wasn't thinking of getting a glass of champagne. It was a scary moment. Storms are violent. They don't have respect for your pedigree, foundation, achievements, or family tree.

Storms often come unexpectedly. They come suddenly at a time of comfort. Storms take options away from you. '*When the storms of life come, the wicked are whirled away, but the godly have a lasting foundation*' (Proverbs 10:25 NLT). The outcome of your exposure to a storm depends on your foundation. If you have watched documentaries on hurricanes and other tropical winds, you will find out that houses with a strong foundation remain standing why those with rickety foundations get swept away. Foundation is the load-bearing part of a building. Your root determines everything. Storms are inevitable but peace in the midst of the storm is optional.

Peace is the product of your confidence in your foundation. There was the story of a little girl who was on a ship that was about to capsize. The captain had advised everybody to jump ship but there was this little girl who was playing with her doll in her room. She was oblivious of what was happening. One of the stewardesses came to her to ask her to avoid the imminent danger. The girl said she had nothing to worry about because her dad was the captain of the ship. Her confidence in her foundation kept her at peace. This is the same kind of confidence you exude when, for instance, you are stopped by the police and you know a high-ranking officer in the police force.

Peace is guaranteed by your relationship. When you have a close relationship with someone who matters in that area of peace, you are not moved. You are comfortable in your skin, you remain comfortable. Peace is not the absence of the storm. Peace is calm in the midst of the storm. God didn't assure us that there won't be storms. Peace helps you to face your fear.

Mary was worried if her marriage would pull through seeing she was now pregnant supernaturally but she received the peace of God by the Word of God. God assured Abraham that he will be a father of many nations. People who lack peace are unsettled. They move from place to place looking for solutions to their problems.

You cannot appropriate God's peace in the storm if you do not recognise His presence with you. You may be in a tight space, under pressure but if you can see God in your storm, you will experience peace. Elisha's servant was shaken when he saw the army that was against them. The servant was surprised that Elisha was unshaken. God asked that the servant's eyes be opened, and he saw the innumerable company of angels that was with them so much that he realised that those who were with them were more than those against them. God allows us to pass through some difficulty for greater glory. If you leave the furnace too soon, you won't be malleable enough for what God has prepared for you.

'My presence shall go with thee and I will give you rest (Exodus 33:14) This was God's response to Moses who needed reassurance that, indeed, he was meant to lead the Israelites out of Egypt. The Israelites were surrounded by difficulty on every side as they journeyed to the Promised Land but God assured Moses of His presence with them. Only God's presence guarantees peace. *'Yea, though I walk through the valley of the shadow of death, I shall fear no evil: for thou art with me...'* (Psalms 23:4). We are at rest when we are confident about God's presence with us. Many of us focus so much on the storm that we fail to recognise that God is present with us.

Jesus told Peter to come to Him on the water and Peter started walking towards Jesus on the water until he looked at the storm around him and began to sink. A prayer you should pray often is that God should help you see Him in the midst of the storm. We sink because we focus on the waves. Rest is conditioned on His presence. If you go alone on your journey in life, you will not last. You've got to go with God and you must be cognizant of His presence.

Three Nevers

1. Never go alone: Whatever God is asking you to do, ask for His presence. Lean not on your own understanding. Lean on God every step of the way. Don't lean on other people's experiences.
2. Never focus on the storm: God is not saying that there won't be storms but don't focus on the storm.
3. Never ignore His instruction: God will tell you to do unconventional things but follow His instruction. This reminds me of when I first came to Australia. I was on a visitor's visa and I had one week left. I had applied for a job but I was rejected by the board. Then God laid it in my heart to go see the Mayor of that same town where I had been rejected. I got access to the Mayor and explained my predicament that I needed a job as a doctor even though I didn't have the required experience. He asked me to tell him about myself and as I shared my story of how I lost my dad and

how I struggled to come to Australia, the Mayor started crying. He asked how he could help me and I asked if he could employ me as an Assistant GP. That was a very weird idea but I assured him it would work.

So, that night, I applied for that post in a way that suits my CV. I took it to him the next day. They processed a bridging visa for me. I didn't finally get the job but during that period, I got the job that God had prepared for me. If I had not taken that bold step to follow the instruction God laid in my heart, I would have missed that opportunity. Just do what God has laid in your heart.

THE BATTLE IS GOD'S

'And it came to pass, when Joshua was by Jericho, that he lifted his eyes and looked and behold, there stood a man over against him with his sword drawn in his hand: and Joshua went unto him, and said unto him, Art thou for us, or for our adversaries? And he said, Nay: but as captain of the host of the LORD am I now come. And Joshua fell on his face to the earth, and did worship, and said unto him, What saith my lord unto his servant'? (Joshua 5:13-14)

Joshua was leading the Israelites to the Promised Land, but there was Jericho before them as an obstacle. So, he needed to strategise on how they would conquer. While he was at this, Joshua lifted his eyes and saw a man who had his sword drawn. This was the pre-incarnate Jesus who appeared to Joshua because of the kind of battle that was ahead of him. The Jericho battle was a different kind of battle. Jesus came as the Captain of the hosts of the Lord. Who was the host or army He referred to here, angels? No! Jesus was referring to the army with Joshua and presented Himself as the Captain to let Joshua know that he wasn't in charge, He was.

This is what we call divine interruption. Jesus showed up to let Joshua know that this battle was His. The strategy that delivered Ai, Amalekites, etc. into his hand wasn't going to suffice here. Jesus was ready to do it His way. And what was Joshua's response? He immediately fell on his face to the ground. Despite his achievements so far, Joshua submitted in worship to God. Joshua didn't argue with God.

Some of us have been trying all kinds of methods to win certain battles when all we need to do is surrender to the Lord. Jesus is in charge. You will not get divine strategy until you totally submit yourself to His will. The battle of Jericho is different because it is won by divine strategy. Why not submit to God?

The wall of Jericho crumbled because Joshua met with the Lord. He gave a strategy to have worshippers march ahead of the soldiers with their trumpets once every day. No one was required to do anything or say anything other than just march around the wall. That didn't make any sense. The battle of Jericho is won by unconventional methods. They obeyed God's instruction and shouted on the seventh day after they had matched around the city seven times. The army of the earth activated the army of heaven through their obedience. It was in that place of worship (falling flat before God) that Joshua received the strategy that got the walls to crumble. You need to surrender to God to help you see how to go about your battle.

Vitória É Certa | Niyi Borire

6

PRAISE

When we praise God, we move God to touch us. Praise can throw confusion into the camp of the enemy and grant us victory. '*Blessed is the people that know the joyful sound: they shall walk, O LORD, in the light of your countenance. In thine name shall they rejoice all the day: and in thine righteousness shall they be exalted.*' (Psalms 89:15-16)

'*And Jehosaphat boweth his head with his face to the ground: and all Judah and the inhabitants of Jerusalem fell before the LORD, worshipping the LORD. And the levites, of the children of the Kohathites, and of the children of the Korhites, stood up to praise the LORD God of Israel with a loud voice on high. And they rose early in the morning, and went forth into the wilderness of Tekoa: and as they went forth, Jehoshaphat stood and said,*

Vitória É Certa | Niyi Borire

Hear me, O Judah, and ye inhabitants of Jerusalem; Believe in the LORD your God, so shall ye be established; believe his prophets, so shall ye prosper. And when he had consulted with the people, he appointed singers unto the LORD, and that should praise the beauty of holiness, as they went out before the army, and to say, Praise the LORD; for his mercy endureth for ever. And when they began to sing and to praise, the LORD set ambushments against the children of Ammon, Moab, and mount Seir, which were come against Judah; and they were smitten.' (2 Chronicles 20:18-22)

How do we win through praise or praise to win?

1. Prayer: Praising God is not just singing. Praising God occurs in prayer. When you talk to God, you praise Him.
2. Reflection: We reflect on God's work. Praise cannot be praise if you are not reflecting on the works of God. You need to reflect on God's kindness, goodness, mercy, love, etc. *'I will meditate also of all thy work, and talk of thy doings'* (Psalms 77:12). Heartfelt praise is built on the foundation of reflection and remembrance.
3. Adoration: When you adore someone, it means you have deep love and respect for them. When we think about what God has done, it should

strengthen our deep love and respect for God. It comes from a place of admiration. When you adore someone, it's not for what they have done (that's gratitude) but for who they are. Adoration is done looking outwards.

4. Introspection: This means soul searching or self-analysis. We are wowed by God's glory and goodness in the place of praise which leads us to look at ourselves and how unworthy or unqualified we are of His goodness. We suddenly realise that we are nothing without Him. It dawns on us that He is the one who gives us our value. Introspection is done looking inwards.

5. Singing: Sometimes, we reduce praise to singing. Praise is more than singing. Paul and Silas praised God through singing in the prison and they activated the power of God. It is good to sing praises to God.

6. Emotional Connection: How can you praise God without an emotional connection? Luke 7:37-38 narrates the story of a woman who was tagged a sinner that found her way into the Pharisee's house where Jesus was. She came with an expensive ointment to lavish on Jesus' feet and as she did, she was crying. Why was she crying? When you see the greatness of God in comparison

with your nothingness, it breaks you down. She understood her unworthiness but she worshipped Him all the same.

7

CONCLUSION: THE VICTORY THAT OVERCOMES

The victory that overcomes does not exist alone. *'For whatever is born of God overcomes the world, this is the victory that overcomes the world even our faith'* (1 John 5:4). For victory to occur or be meaningful, there has to be the victor (which is you) and the vanquished (the world). The word *world* is from the Greek word *Cosmos* which means an orderly or harmonious arrangement of things or a well-crafted system that has a specific goal in mind. The word *Cosmos*

has different contexts in the scriptures. It is used to refer to the following:

1. Universe: This refers to the body of planets, stars, and galaxies.
2. Inhabitants of the earth: This refers to the human race. John 3:16 explains this; *'For God so loved the world that He gave His only begotten son that whosoever believes in him should not perish but have everlasting life.'* The world in this context is referring to the whole of humankind.
3. The ungodly multitude: This refers to the whole mass of men who are alienated from God and therefore antagonistic to the course of Christ. *'If ye were of the world, the world would love his own: but because ye are not of the world, but I have chosen you out of the world, therefore the world hateth you.'* (John 15:19) Here, Jesus was not referring to the elements but the mass of people who are in opposition to the course of Christ. *'Ye are of God, little children, and have overcome them: because greater is he that is in you, than he that is in the world. They are of the world: therefore speak they of the world, and the world heareth them.'* (1 John 4:4-5). They are men and women who do not

reckon with God.

4. The whole circle of earthly goods: This refers to all earthly endowments, pleasure, riches, advantages, achievements, etc. which are temporal, fleeting, and ephemeral. This cosmos, though not of any eternal value, can still seduce people away from God and hinder them from serving. '*And we know that we are of God, and the whole world lieth in wickedness*'. (1 John 5:19)

Having established these different applications of *Cosmos*, when we talk about the victory that overcomes the world, we are talking about the system of things that is orderly arranged to antagonise the course of Christ. This system is designed to subjugate its occupants without their perception. The world operates to keep the inhabitants unaware of their predicaments. It's a subtle influence on the mind of man so that he lives contrary to the course of Christ. The world has a way of subtly conditioning man. It happens subconsciously. The world appeals to the flesh. The world system appeals to the crudeness and unrefined nature of man. It seeks to subvert and invert the perception of man. The system of the world slowly adjusts the perception of men such that what used to be wrong is now right, whether pop culture, sexuality, comportment, attitude, etc.

Vitória É Certa | Niyi Borire

The world has inverted the judgement of man. The world system is more powerful than a single individual. It doesn't matter how talented, educated, or sophisticated a man is, he is susceptible by nature to the influence of the world. It is like the gravitational force that pulls everything to the middle of the earth. This force of the world is spiritual and contrary to the course of Christ. *'And I sought for a man among them, that should make up the hedge, and stand in the gap before me for the land, that I should not destroy it: but I found none'.* Ezekiel 22:30

God is still looking for men that will rise above the roaring waves of worldly influence. The world system has the iceberg effect, the principle that explains that what is evident or seen is often smaller than what it really is. A typical iceberg (that is seen on the surface) is way bigger underneath than what is seen on the surface of the water. So, one may mistakenly refer to an iceberg as a small structure. However, it is deeper and more dangerous underneath. The same is true for the world system. On the surface, it looks harmless and encouraging (the culture, music, lifestyle, etc.), however, the spiritual backing of the world system underneath is very dangerous. There is a spiritual worldly system at work that is constantly enticing the children of God. The devil is no longer dressed in red clothes with horns that we were used to seeing in cartoon illustrations of him in the earlier days. The devil is now well-dressed and well-blended into the church.

This reminds me of the story of how the Eskimos captured wolves. They used the skin of wolves as their clothes (because it is usually very thick and can protect against cold) while they ate their meat as food. The way the Eskimos capture these wolves is to freeze the blood of another animal on a knife or double-edged sword, then they drop it in the open ice. A wolf can smell the blood from kilometres away, so it traces the blood smell and once it locates it, it begins to lick the blood off the ice like a lollipop which is usually very sweet. The wolf licks on until its tongue is cut by the sharp knife. A laceration on the tongue is a deadly thing for a wolf. It will eventually bleed to death. It may take a few hours or even days but the Eskimos, who are hiding somewhere around where the bait was put, will patiently wait until the wolf drops dead. This is exactly how the devil uses the world system to capture Christians. A wounded soldier becomes a useless soldier.

The worldly system promotes sin and sinners that usually gets us envious. The popularity that the world system gives its stars who are parading everywhere on social media can get believers hooked. Advertisers play on the natural inclination of men and women to love the world. There are a lot of advertising campaigns that naturally appeal to our base/crude desires.

How Can We Overcome the World?

Let's look at 1 John 5:4 again in some other translations:

'For every child of God defeats this world, and we achieve this victory through our faith' (NLT)

'For everyone born of God overcomes the world. This is the victory that has overcome the world – our faith'. (NIV)

'For everyone born of God is victorious and overcomes the world; and this is the victory that has conquered and overcome the world – our [continuing, persistent] faith [in Jesus the Son of God]'. (AMP)

All of these translations emphasise something – every single child of God overcomes the world. There is hope and assurance that once you are in union with Christ, your victory is certain. The title of being an overcomer comes the moment you enter a relationship with God. The way you escape the centripetal force of the world system is to come into a relationship with God through the acceptance of Jesus Christ into your heart.

No matter the socio-economic status or achievements, a man by nature cannot achieve this victory by himself.

To overcome means to bridle and subdue (it means you control how something manifests or behaves. When you bridle something, you are able to control it just like a horse rider controls a horse with the bits and reins attached to the headgear of the horse), master and conquer, beat and defeat, overpower and overwhelm, quell and crush, trounce and trash, outclass and out trip.

You cannot overcome something that you are not in contact with. You cannot overcome the world and its system that you are not existing in. Defeating the world is only possible through contact. You can't subdue the worldly system in isolation. God didn't ask us to live our lives like monks who hide themselves away in monasteries away from the influence of the world. God didn't design us to hide away from the world. He wants us to shine. *'And the light shineth in darkness; and the darkness comprehended it not'*. (John 1:5). Notice that the light shines in darkness not out of the darkness. Light can only influence the dark when they come together.

God did not call us to a life of isolation but separation. Separation doesn't mean avoidance of contact. It means overcoming despite contact. It means standing out despite contact. Separation was what happened to Shadrack, Meshach, and Abednego who refused to bow to the idol Nebuchaddenazer put up. They were able to stand their ground and got the victory in the end even though they were thrown into the furnace of fire. That is how we shine through the darkness around us today too. To overcome is to stand out despite contact.

One of the major challenges of the COVID-19 global pandemic is social isolation or quarantine because of the risk of infection. We are able to live with Flu, smallpox, etc. today because of the vaccines that have been provided to curtail them. So, even though we live in the midst of them, we are not infected by them if we have been vaccinated. I believe the same will be the case for the COVID-19 virus. This is the same way God inoculates us with His Word so that even though we are exposed to worldly influences, they don't harm us, rather we shine in their midst.

There is a big danger in isolation. It gives us a false sense of security and superiority. There are people who feel secure from the influence of the world by isolating themselves. They don't mingle with people in the name of protecting themselves. This is a reason why a lot of people are not influencing the world today. There can be no impact without contact. Even Jesus understood this. That was why he came as a man even though he was God. He came in the flesh to validate His impact. *'For we have not an high priest which cannot be touched with the feeling of our infirmities; but was in all points tempted like as we are, yet without sin'*. (Hebrews 4:15). Jesus had to go through what we are now going through.

The Pharisees and Sadducees had a false sense of superiority. They felt they were different from the others and carried themselves so. When we have a false sense of superiority, it drains us of love and compassion. We suddenly feel that we are better and the world is so filthy that we fail to see the good that can come out of sinners. To make an impact, we need to be humble. Paul understood this when he said that he became all things to all men so that he could win some. Jesus mingled with sinners. He never tried to be superior. He believed that it is only sick people that need a physician. If the world is sick and in need of healing, who else will bring God's healing to them if not we (as believers)? We cannot do this in isolation. If we do this, we will die without impacting our world.

Vitória É Certa | Niyi Borire

I will love to share a quote from Ray Stedman's sermon; *'There comes a marked tendency to withdraw, to seek our own crowd, to create our own little separate world -- a world that is as complete as we can make it, with recreation, and education, and all that we need from the cradle to the grave. We create our own smug, airtight circle in which we live, and which we have set up to run competition to the "worldly" world outside.*

Now, ultimately, that kind of thinking produced the monasteries that appeared in the Middle Ages. Men decided that the way to avoid the temptations of the world was to completely seclude themselves from it, so they built high-walled monasteries and lived their lives inside, and thus sought to avoid the world.

Today we do not build walls of brick and mortar in order to avoid these things, but we still have walls of thought and seclusion that are almost equally effective. In this way, we become 20th century monks, doing this very same thing. And the worst tragedy of all, in my estimation, is that we are passing all this on to our young people. We are handing along these conceptions, as they pick up our way of life and our way of thinking. Instead of teaching them to overcome evil, we are teaching them to avoid it. They are not learning how to fight the good fight of faith. We do not know how to fight it ourselves, many of us, so how can we tell them? How can we show them?

To sum up, the Christian's vocation is to be in the world, but not of it; to represent Christ in it and to intercede on its behalf because it is under judgment (this is the Christian's priesthood), to identify himself with its sufferings but not with its attitudes, to bring his influence to bear upon the world's life without being corrupted by the world's ways; to stand on the frontier, holding forth the Word of Life, and so to love and obey that Word that he has been delivered from the evil one and sanctified in the truth. Such a calling involves a cross. The man who separates himself from the world and seeks to escape it does not know the cross. The man who submits to the world's pressures and loses his distinctiveness as a Christian does not know that cross. The man who seeks to be in the world, as our Lord was in it, but shows that he is not of it because he is a Christian and in Christ; that man will find his cross. It's only the disciple who follows Christ in both these respects who has a cross to take up'.

Vitória É Certa | Niyi Borire

How Can We Achieve This Victory That Overcomes the World?

We have seen from 1 John 5:4 that being born of God gives you the status of an overcomer, however, you still need to grab a hold of this victory. You still need to appropriate this victory. You still need to claim it. A cheque is worthless if you can't go to the bank to claim it. The cheque you need to walk in victory daily is your faith. This victory cannot be achieved by your efforts or in isolation. It comes only through faith.

The fuel that sustains the flames of victory is faith. When faith dries up, the flames of victory dissipate. Faith is the channel through which the grace of God flows. This grace is what sustains our victory. When you are born of God by accepting that Jesus is Lord, then you can be sure of victory.

Our daily dependence on God – faith – is what assures consistent victory. You need to learn to trust God daily. I learnt faith while I was in college and we had nothing. My dad lost his business and his marriage was almost breaking down as well in that season and things became really tough. I was a first-year student in college and getting to school daily was difficult. I had a small plastic bag with my books and I would frequently knock on our neighbours' doors daily to ask for help. There were two women in particular who always helped with little money. There were days when I would get favoured by the bus driver. At break time, I would go to the cafeteria hoping to get food and someone would just pay for me. Somehow, for a whole year, God kept sustaining me. This built a lot of confidence in me. It has become a reference point in my life till now that God can always come through for me even in difficult times. Faith helps you to trust God.

Faith without trust or hope is not faith. Trust is the deliberate choice you make to depend on someone. Faith without trust is just a mere mental assent. It is putting your weight on what God's Word has said. I love the way Mike Todd illustrated faith in one of his messages. He brought out a small wooden chair and asked one of his congregants (who was very fat) to sit on the chair. The man was hesitant when he realised that his weight was more than the chair could support. Mike asked the man if he believed that the weight could support his weight. The man said yes but remained hesitant to sit on the chair. He wasn't ready to commit to it. Until you are ready to commit your life to what you believe, it is not faith. You have got to believe God with your life. You need to become like Ruth who was willing to follow Naomi even when she wasn't certain of what the future held for her. '*And blessed is she that believed: for there shall be a performance of those things which were told her from the Lord*'. (Luke 1:45)

I read the story of Charles Blondin and Harry Colcord. Charles was a tightrope walker who was known for crossing the Niagara Gorge river. The remarkable thing about this man after being the first person to cross this river in 1859 is that his manager, Harry Colcord, decided one day to be a part of the act. This is because over the years, Charles had walked several times with several styles over that river and people pay so much to watch him. It was even recorded that he cooked an omelette on one of his trips on the tightrope. One day, he wanted to do something unusual. He needed someone he could carry on his back across the Niagara Gorge which had America on one side and Canada on the other side. He found no one but his manager, Harry Colcord. He carried his manager across the rope.

It was recorded that Harry was scared even though Charles was not. At one point, Charles said, '*Look up, Harry. You are no longer Colcord but Blondin. Until I clear this pace, be a part of me, mind, body, and soul. If I sway, sway with me. Do not attempt to do any balancing yourself*'. Harry did exactly as he was told.

Vitória É Certa | Niyi Borire

When Charles swayed, Harry swayed. When Charles moved, Harry moved. That was trust in display. The spectators had seen Charles do all kinds of amazing things in the past on the tightrope like pushing a wheelbarrow, walking with a blindfold, walking backwards on the rope, doing backflips, etc. but no one was ready to subject themselves to the experiment of being carried on Charles' back. Harry was ready to put his money where his mouth was. This is the difference between knowing God can and God will. It's not enough to know that God can, you must put everything on the line because you know that He will.

www.ingramcontent.com/pod-product-compliance
Lightning Source LLC
Chambersburg PA
CBHW031256290426
44109CB00012B/606